SAINTS FOR KIDS BY KIDS

Father Robert Charlebois
Mary Sue Holden
Marilyn Diggs Mange

LIGUORI
PUBLICATIONS

One Liguori Drive
Liguori, Missouri 63057
(314) 464-2500

Imprimi Potest:
John F. Dowd, C.SS.R.
Provincial, St. Louis Province
Redemptorist Fathers

Imprimatur:
+ Edward J. O'Donnell
Vicar General, Archdiocese of St. Louis

ISBN 0-89243-223-3
Library of Congress Catalog Card Number: 84-82121

Contents

Acknowledgments

Grown-ups Who Helped
and Kids Who Created

It is with deep appreciation and gratitude that we recognize the many wonderful people who contributed to making this book come to be.

To *Father Thomas Gileece,* of the New York Archdiocesan Department of Education, who served as our theologian and counselor. You had the mammoth job of reviewing over a year's worth of material, and you never once complained. For reading and commenting on every last word, and for steering us in the right direction, thank you.

To *Monsignor Eugene V. Clark,* for your wonderful encouragement, advice, and conviction that a book of saints for kids, by kids, was not only a really good idea but also a necessity. We thank you for keeping our momentum going.

To the *Reverend Martin Seeley,* for providing us with countless books and research materials, which greatly reduced the amount of legwork and library hours we needed to get the job done.

To *Penny Mann,* who believed in this project and devoted many a Sunday School class to this book. Thank you for all those Sunday mornings when you brought us together with children in a casual, comfortable setting.

To *Audrey Kolberg,* who helped us focus on creative research approaches in the classroom. Your invaluable advice enabled us to ask the right questions at the right time. Thanks to you, the children were happy to see us again and again. Never once did they suspect that writing a book was work. They always thought we were having fun.

To the school principals who gave us a chance and allowed us to interrupt busy classroom schedules: *Sister Miriam Helen*

Callahan of St. Ignatius Loyola, *Sister Virginia Chiambalero* of St. Catherine of Siena, and *Sister John Marie* of St. Stephen of Hungary. Thanks again for your patience and support.

To each and every teacher who willingly surrendered classroom time to conduct this project, we extend a special note of thanks; from St. Catherine of Siena: *Miss Andrea Hamilton, Miss Carolyn Howard, Mr. Joseph Salerno;* from St. Ignatius Loyola: *Sister Bernard Quinn, Sister Frances Smith, Mrs. Mary Ann Lyons, Mrs. Florence Rebovich, Sister Frances Bones, Miss Susan Cienki;* from St. Stephen of Hungary: *Sister M. Judith, Mrs. Carol O'Connor, Mrs. Sandra Davis,* and *Mr. Lawrence Greiner.*

To *God* for making this book a nonfiction and for providing us all with a real live cast of characters.

To *the saints,* our superheroes, without whom this book would not have been possible. Thank you for your truly wonderful examples and for showing us human ways to obtain our heavenly goal.

Last and foremost, to *all the terrific kids* for and by whom this book was written. We not only thank you — we salute you. We told you some simple stories, and you responded with a creation. We brought you a gigantic challenge, and you opened up your hearts and minds to meet it. It is to you that this book is dedicated with love, admiration, and our profound respect.

A Word to Grown-ups

How This Book Was Written

Let's face it. Kids love to talk to other kids. What do they talk about? They cover quite a range of subjects, but one of their favorite topics is SUPERHEROES.

Everyone has heard of Superman, Spiderman, and Wonder Woman. But how many children today have heard of the Wonder Worker, Saint Anthony of Padua? The commercial superheroes of TV, comic books, and mass media have taken the place of some other superheroes who have the potential of being just as exciting, if not more so! Real-life saints, the traditional superheroes of the Church, can be more stimulating than fantasy images if they are presented in the right way.

The intent of this book is to capture children's imaginations by bringing the saints down from pedestals in church and into the children's everyday world. The children can then see the saints as friends rather than as untouchable, inaccessible holy persons. The children can come to the point where they will talk with the saints or call upon them for favors in times of need.

This goal poses a challenge, however. How do we present saints as "buddies" and yet retain the holiness and heroism that makes them saints?

Success in meeting this challenge lies in the way the stories are told. It goes like this. The children first see a saint as a kid with all the "imperfections" or troubles that they themselves may be experiencing. They then follow the saint as he or she grows into a holy person. As they come to know the saint better, they feel admiration mixed with a "they-know-what-I-am-going-through" sort of closeness.

As children can tell you, nobody tells a story to a child better than another child. That is why we composed this book in such a way that children actually took part in its creation. This was done by entering schoolrooms and Sunday School classes and

7

telling stories of particular saints to the children. The children, in turn, would then retell the stories in their own words. Discussions would follow in which we asked such things as "How would you feel if you were in his shoes?" or "What do you suppose this saint would pray to God?" The children's responses, both verbal and pictorial, were then edited and incorporated into this collection of stories, prayers, and drawings. This approach allowed us to enter into the children's minds.

Choosing which saints would appear in this book was no easy task. Extensive research went into selecting a balance of saints based upon deeds, nationality, sex, and time in history. Violence and martyrdom were kept to a minimum. We started with twenty saints and picked the eight with whom the children found it easiest to relate. The result, in some cases, was rather surprising. Of the eight saints chosen, only two of them have any obvious connection with children's experience: Saint Nicholas, who is associated with Santa Claus, and Saint Patrick, whose day is celebrated annually.

After our library research, followed by the extensive participation of some 300 students in the actual re-creation of the stories and drawings, we went back to the classrooms and Sunday School classes to get some feedback. We asked the children: How do you feel about a book written for you by other children? Like all kids, they thought it was terrific because, as one fifth grader put it, "Kids say it best!"

"Those kids talk like they know the saint, like they are friends or something!"

"All we hear all day is adults talking to us. It's great to have a book by other kids."

Children need the opportunity to express themselves. They enjoy having a hand in the production of their own reading material. Our book provides this outlet, a book for children, created by children. The result is *Saints for Kids by Kids,* told simply and honestly as only children can tell it.

A Word to Kids

What Does It Take to Be a Saint, Anyway?

God doesn't just pick out certain people to be saints and nobody else. After all, everybody is special to Him, right? I mean, I feel special. Don't you? God wants everybody to be good so I guess He wants everybody to be a saint.

Well, then, why are some people saints and not others? What exactly is a saint?

I'll bet they were a lot like you and me. They were real people with real feelings, with real problems. Just like me. They all lived on the planet Earth. Just like me. When they were kids. . . .

Some saints were really poor, some were rich.

Some were beautiful, some were average.

Some were skinny, some were fat.

Some were shy, some were forward.

Some were smart, some not as smart.

Some went to school, some were uneducated.

Some were healthy, some were sickly.

Some behaved, some were troublemakers.

Some were popular, some simply got on people's nerves.

Saints weren't born perfect. Nobody is perfect. They didn't walk around with halos over their heads. That would be kind of weird, don't you think? No, I think that saints started out just like the rest of us — the hard way.

But something must have happened to make the saints stand out from the rest of us. Since God wants everybody to be a saint, maybe they just listened better. Maybe when He called, they heard — or something like that.

If you really look at saints, they had a few things in common. For instance, they were always talking to God. That's called praying. And they always wanted to make God happy because they loved Him so much. They weren't just thinking about themselves all the time. They were thinking about what God wanted them to do.

Some of the saints were good thinkers, so those saints would write about religion or teach. Some saints were good workers, so they would lend a helping hand to the poor and elderly. Some were rich, so they would give away money and things to the needy.

I don't know, but I guess it's really hard to be a saint. I mean, I wouldn't like to give all my stuff away. And I'm always busy with things to do. I try to do what I should, but sometimes things happen and I make mistakes. I try, but I'm no saint — not yet, anyway.

I like hearing about the saints, though. We can learn a lot from their examples. They teach us how to be closer to God. And they show us how to stay on the right track. They help to correct some of the bad things that go on. That's why God gives them special powers. You know, they get to make miracles happen.

So, if we pray to them for things, they listen. Saints are definitely good listeners. They are like our special friends in heaven. They know what it's like down here, and they can help us get up there.

THE
SAINTS

1
Saint Thomas Aquinas

When Saint Thomas was a little boy, he was tall and bulky, so he walked around awkwardly. He seemed to grow a whole lot faster than other kids his age, and that made him a bit clumsy. Sometimes he tripped over things or bumped into people. His classmates would make fun of him. That must have hurt.

If it bothered Thomas to be the object of jokes, he never let it show. I guess he would just hang down his head and look at the ground, pretending not to notice. He never said anything about it. He just held it inside.

But there was one thing that really shook Saint Thomas up. He was scared of thunderstorms. Every time one started he would run to the nearest church for cover.

It all started one dark and stormy night. Saint Thomas and his little sister were asleep in their beds. They shared a room, and her bed was close to the window.

All of a sudden, the sky streaked with lightning bolts. The booming thunder pounded endlessly. Thomas was restless that night as he sat up in bed. Huge flashes of lightning were getting closer and closer. It was almost as if Thomas could just reach out and touch one. Then it happened. One quick bolt hit his sister's bed and she died instantly, right before his eyes. I guess Saint Thomas must have screamed his head off. It was a memory that would stay with him the rest of his life. From that night on, every time there was a thunderstorm Saint Thomas would break out in a cold sweat and pray.

He probably said something like, "Oh God, I know this is stupid, but I can't take these thunderstorms. Please stay with me awhile."

Saint Thomas was always praying because he liked to talk with God. Maybe that's why other people thought he wasn't very smart. He didn't have much to say out loud because his thoughts were always silently directed to our Lord.

Anyhow, when Saint Thomas grew up he decided to be a priest. After he discussed it with his mother, she thought it was a wonderful idea. "Oh, this is fabulous news!" she said. "You are going to be a Benedictine monk, and they are so important. I can't wait to tell everybody."

"No, Mom, you misunderstood," Saint Thomas quickly answered. "I don't want to be a Benedictine monk; I want to join the Dominicans."

"That will never happen, Thomas," his mother replied. "The Dominicans are nothing more than poor, penniless beggars. No son of mine will end up like that, and you should know better."

All Saint Thomas knew was that he really wanted to join the humble Order of Dominicans who were poor preachers. He didn't want to upset his mother, but he had to do what he thought was right. The next day he ran away to follow his conscience.

When his mother found out, she was more than upset. She was furious. "How dare he go against my wishes!" she thought. Summoning Saint Thomas's older brother, a soldier, the angry mother asked him to track down Saint Thomas and bring him home immediately. Taking a small army of men, his brother found Saint Thomas hitchhiking on the road to the Dominican seminary.

"You're in trouble now," the soldier said, as he forced his younger brother home. "Why couldn't you

have waited? Maybe, in time, Mother would give in and let you do what you want.''

Saint Thomas said nothing. All he wanted to do was serve God as a humble priest. Now here he was being kidnapped and taken back to his house like a prisoner.

Saint Thomas was kept at home like that for two whole years. During this time his mother calmed down and tried to make it up to her son. She bought him nice clothes and organized parties in his honor. But Saint Thomas looked as if he was bored with it all. Next, his mother introduced him to pretty girls, hoping he would find a steady girl friend. But that didn't change his mind. He just wanted to leave and join the Order of his choice, the Dominicans. After trying everything she could think of, his mother finally gave in and let him go.

While Saint Thomas was a seminarian studying to be a priest, the jokes about his clutziness started again. Other seminarians laughed and nicknamed him the "Dumb Ox." He was a quiet person, so everybody thought that he was slow — you know, not too bright. Even though he never seemed to fit in, Saint Thomas never insulted anybody back. God must have helped him ignore it. I think I would want to punch those guys out.

As time went on, there was one student who felt sorry for Saint Thomas. The student wanted to find a way to include Thomas as a friend, so the student offered to help Saint Thomas with his homework. It was a funny thing, though, because it didn't work out that way at all. It turned out the other way around. Saint Thomas ended up helping the good student with *his* homework. Saint Thomas's new friend was amazed at how smart he really was. The friend was so surprised that he took the paper he and Saint Thomas were working on and showed it to their teacher. They were working on a very complicated problem — something about Church matters — and Saint Thomas had simplified the answers so that anybody could understand them. When the teacher saw the paper, he wasn't surprised. He said, "You may call Thomas a 'dumb ox,' but someday he will astound the world with how smart he truly is."

At the time, nobody realized it, but Saint Thomas was a genius. He not only grew up to be tall, strong, and handsome; he also grew up to be a leader in Church teachings.

Saint Thomas wrote very important books for God and taught at many universities. In his books, Saint Thomas explained some of the mysteries of the Church and its teachings. He gave good reasons showing that God is real and not just someone people make up in their minds. Nobody else even came close to explaining things as well as Saint Thomas did. His books helped a lot of people to believe. He even wrote some of the hymns we sing in church. I like Saint Thomas because he never thought he was some kind of hotshot, even though he really was a whole lot smarter than anybody else. Funny how people could call someone like that "dumb."

Saint Thomas said he learned more by praying than by studying, and he talked to God every day. When he prayed, rays of light would shine around his head. Maybe that was God's way of talking back.

What would you pray to Saint Thomas for, now that you know him better?

Prayers to Saint Thomas

Dear Saint Thomas, please help me to put up with people who make fun of me or ignore me just because I might not be like them. I know you've been through a lot, and still you have faith that God loves you no matter what. Please help me to be like you. Help me not to show off my intelligence but to keep quiet and not be a snob. Let me be like you.

— Amy

Saint Thomas, I know you've been through everything, so I ask you to help the people that are called names, there's some of them in my class. Sometimes, I'm one of them. I also ask you to help the people that are afraid of things. I am afraid of the dark, and I know many other people that are afraid of things too. So please help them. Thank you.

— Patricia

Saint Thomas, you know what it's like to lose a loved one. Now help us on earth to overcome the pain of losing a loved person in our family.

— Elizabeth

Dear Saint Thomas, please help me understand my math problems. You were always so smart, maybe you could explain it to me.

— Raul

2
Saint Joan
of Arc

When Saint Joan of Arc was a little girl, she was very friendly. Everybody liked her. I guess she was so popular because she always tried to help people. If someone was sick, Saint Joan would always do things to make that person feel better. Sometimes she would even invite poor, tired travelers into her house and put them to sleep in her own bed. Her parents understood because they knew that their daughter had a good heart. Besides, the travelers looked as if they could use a restful sleep.

When Saint Joan was growing up, though, things weren't exactly easy. Everybody wasn't just walking around being happy all the time. It was a time when her whole country, France, was fighting a civil war. France was going under because Frenchmen were killing other Frenchmen. They were all fighting to see who would be king. The stronger side would get to pick the person they wanted. Meanwhile, a lot of people were dying.

Just when France was losing all these lives and losing resources like food and money, another country tried to take advantage of the situation. That country was England.

England sent over a great big army, attempting to overthrow France and conquer it. Yes, France was in bad shape.

Often the invasions hit pretty close to Saint Joan's house. Once the fighting was so bad that her entire family had to run for the hills in the middle of the night. They had to hide in the bushes until it was safe to return to their shattered home.

Saint Joan was really worried about what would happen. She prayed that the fighting and killing would stop soon. It was during such a prayer one day that something very unusual happened.

Saint Joan was only fourteen years old and working in the fields when she heard voices calling her name. "Joan, Joan, Joan," the voices said. Quickly she turned around, expecting to see her mother and father. Instead she only saw a bright light shining in the yard. "Oh well," she probably thought, "I must be hearing things." So she went back to her work.

Again the voices interrupted her chores. "Joan, Joan."

"OK, who is it?" she said. Turning around, she saw three saints: Saint Michael, Saint Catherine, and Saint Margaret.

"We have a message for you," Saint Michael said. "You are supposed to join the army and save France."

"How am I going to do that?" Joan answered. "How am I going to save France?" She knew how to work and help people, but she didn't know how to fight in a war. "It's impossible. No one will take me seriously," she thought.

Then, just as suddenly, the saints disappeared.

Saint Joan tried to forget about the whole thing, but the voices never gave up. The saints were sent by God, and He wanted her to be His soldier for France. Well, if this was what God wanted of her, then she would do her best. Maybe she prayed something like, "Dear God, if you want me to fight, then I'll do it for You. But please make sure we win."

Proudly, Saint Joan told her parents about the voices and that she was expected to fight in the army. Naturally, her mother and father had a hard time believing this story. But Saint Joan insisted that she go away and join the army.

"Absolutely not!" they said. "You're staying right here."

Saint Joan was disappointed that her parents felt this way, but she had to keep her promise to God and the saints. Next she decided to see her uncle and ask for his help.

Her uncle listened carefully to the story and knew that his niece would never make up something so important. He offered to take her secretly to the army where she might enlist.

Seeing the young girl standing in line, the general was not amused. "Are you kidding?" he laughed. "Take this little girl? Humph! No! Girls can't join the army. She would be killed." The general turned to

Saint Joan's uncle and said, "Take her home and give her a good spanking."

When she got home, Saint Joan had a lot of explaining to do. "I'm sorry for just leaving," she said, "but I had to try."

"Joan," her mother pleaded, "please give up this idea. You belong here with us. You are just a little girl."

Frustrated and confused, Saint Joan tried to obey her mother. But the voices kept calling her. "Find a way, Joan, France needs you." They told her to be brave and that God was on her side.

Finally, when she was seventeen years old, Saint Joan ran away to try again. This time she had to get permission from someone of authority at the court. No matter how hard she tried, she couldn't get inside the city hall. No one paid any attention to her, except to make fun of her.

At last, something happened to give Saint Joan the chance she needed. Outside the castle she recognized the king's son talking with a group of soldiers.

Forcing her way past the crowd, Saint Joan ran up to the prince and begged him to listen to her. The good prince was impressed with her courage and, with God's help, he believed everything she told him. Immediately, the prince gave his permission for Saint Joan to join the army. From that moment on, Saint Joan's life was changed forever.

Because she was obviously a girl, Saint Joan thought her long brown hair would attract too much attention. So she cut it all off to look more like a boy. Her battalion gave her a suit of clothes, and she wore white armor. Now she was ready for battle.

Imagine, a young girl facing an enemy so mean that she could die at any moment. Saint Joan of Arc knew she might die, but she tried not to let her fear show. She was scared, but she was also filled with the grace of the Holy Spirit, so she rode proudly.

Seeing the way she faced the enemy, the fighting men of France started to place their trust in Saint Joan. Stories of her courage spread throughout the land. Soon they had new hope as they shouted, "With Joan on our side we can't lose. God has sent her to help us." Now the army fought harder and stronger than ever before.

While Saint Joan was in the army she fought in many, many battles and won almost all of them. She rode at the head of the army, not so much to actually fight but to stand as a heroic symbol of encouragement. Sometimes she got wounded, and the French soldiers took good care of her. They always tried to protect her. Just by having her around, the French soldiers knew they would win. They knew that they were going to beat the English and get them out of their country forever. And they did.

Saint Joan also helped her friend, the prince, to become the next king of France. That brought the whole country together, and France was no longer divided.

But before the war ended, the voices she had heard earlier came back and spoke to Saint Joan again. The voices said: "Joan, you are not going to live much longer."

All too soon, enemies of Saint Joan captured her and sold her to England.

Questioning her over and over again, some people refused to believe that she actually talked with the saints. "You're making the whole thing up," they shouted. "Tell the truth. We know you are lying."

Although Saint Joan was exhausted, she told them that the saints really did talk to her and that God wanted her to be His soldier for France.

One high minister said, "Why would God have a message for a little girl like you and not an important minister like me? Tell me that the saints didn't talk to you, or else we will kill you."

Saint Joan could only tell him what she had said before. "I cannot tell you what you want to hear. I will not lie. God did give me a message and I obeyed."

"The saints didn't talk to you," he said. "It was the devil. Now you will burn for your lies."

The trial was over, and the jury called Joan a witch. She was sentenced to die. Then she was dragged to the marketplace and burned at the stake.

So, at the young age of nineteen, Saint Joan of Arc died at the hands of her enemies. To this day, the French honor Joan of Arc as a heroine, and they remember her as their most famous saint. She trusted God and did what was asked of her. She saved France.

What would you pray to Saint Joan of Arc for, now that you know her better?

Prayers to Saint Joan of Arc

Dear Saint Joan, I wish I could be more like you.
Please help me to have courage enough to fight for
what I believe in. I admire the way you told the truth
even though they were going to kill you.

— Michael

Dear Saint Joan,
   Give me strength.
   You have a lot of strength.
   You were only nineteen
   You died so young
   But you did not lie,
   That is the greatest thing.
   You are soft and gentle
   Just like a dove.
   You believed in God
   And you died because of your faith and love.
   Our great Saint Joan.

— Kim

Dear Saint Joan of Arc, I wish that more people in the
world would be just like you. You are so brave and you
did not lie. Maybe if more people would be like you,
the world would be a better place.

— La-Tanya

Dear Saint Joan, please help stop all the wars around
the world. If only there could be peace on the earth
and everyone would love each other. Please try. Thank
you.

— Margaret

3
Saint Patrick

When Saint Patrick was a little boy, he wasn't very saintly. Before he was a saint he had no regard for religion, and he didn't think about God very much. Whenever his family went to Mass on Sunday, Saint Patrick used to act up. He would squirm around and talk and make a nuisance of himself. He was bored. I guess he didn't know what you're supposed to do in church. He got on everybody's nerves.

Saint Patrick never thought he would grow up to be a saint, but somehow he did. You see, God wanted him to.

One day he was walking around and a bunch of pirates kidnapped him. He lived in England, and the pirates were going to make him a slave in Ireland. In those days pirates were always stealing people so they could sell them back to their families for ransom or sell them as slaves to somebody else. I guess that's how some pirates made their living.

Anyhow, they tied Saint Patrick up and threw him in the bottom of a boat. Saint Patrick wasn't the only one. There were a lot of people, grown-ups and kids, in the same bad situation. Everybody was scared. They didn't know what was going on or what would happen to them next. While Saint Patrick was there he didn't feel like jumping around the way he used to, even though there were other kids in the boat.

That's when Saint Patrick started praying to God, like he should have done when he was in church. He probably said something like, "God, I'm having a real rough time, and I need someone to help me. I really don't have any friends, so I need to talk to you. Please God, I really wish You would help me out of this." And as the long, hard journey continued, Saint Patrick prayed, "Why did this have to happen to me, God?" Day by day, Saint Patrick's faith deepened, and he was drawn closer to our Lord.

At last, the ship docked in Ireland. It was a strange country. The people there spoke a language Saint Patrick had never heard before. He felt out of place. The pirates sold him to a rancher. He became a slave, and his master made him work very hard. All the time, Saint Patrick talked with God and he felt peaceful, even though he missed his family and friends.

Then one day when he was taking a nap, God told Patrick to escape and go to England. When he woke up, Saint Patrick remembered the dream, but he was afraid. "If I run away, my master will kill me."

But Saint Patrick wanted to please God, so he ran away. He had to walk 200 miles to reach a boat. It's hard to walk 200 miles on foot. If you took a car, you would get there in four hours. If you think that's a long time, it probably took Saint Patrick a month or more. He had to beg for his food, trying to find someone kind and friendly. I'll bet his feet got real sore.

At the end of his long journey, Saint Patrick approached a sea captain and asked to catch a ride. The captain laughed and said, "No."

Saint Patrick went on begging the captain. "I'll work real hard for you to pay my way," he promised.

But the captain still said, "No."

Saint Patrick started to turn and walk away as he prayed, "Please help me, God. I have to make this trip."

Just then the captain thought it over and changed his mind. He said, "OK, kid, you can come aboard."

So they sailed around until they finally saw a shore.
It was a place called Gaul, but they thought it was
England. Once they got on shore, they noticed that
there was nobody around. For days they roamed
around, until finally they ran out of food. Pretty soon
they were starving.

Finally, Saint Patrick told everybody to stop griping
and pray. Once again God helped him out. All of a

sudden a bunch of pigs came running right out in front of them. Everyone was happy because they had ham for dinner.

Shortly afterward, they got back on the boat and sailed for England. Saint Patrick was so happy because he found his family. His mother said, "I never want you to leave me again."

Saint Patrick studied the Bible and became a priest. Then he started getting messages again, like the time God told him to escape to England. He heard voices of people he had known in Ireland, telling him to return there. God needed his help. The last thing he wanted to do was go back to Ireland. But, if God wanted him to go, then he would risk his life if he had to.

Because Saint Patrick was now a priest, he wanted to see the Pope and ask his permission to go to Ireland. He told the Pope that he wanted to teach the Irish people about God and the Church. But the Pope said, "That's a rough place, Ireland. It's dangerous, and they hate the Christian religion."

But, not to disappoint him, the Pope finally said, "OK, you can go." God must have inspired the Pope to say that.

Saint Patrick had to be very careful. He was definitely afraid. The warlords forced everybody to do what they wanted. You had to live by their rules, or else they'd kill you, just like that. I think the warlords must have been pretty bad people. They made everybody else do all the work, while they just sat around and gambled and drank.

Anyhow, Saint Patrick tried to show the people a new way to live by loving God. He was always generous. He helped the poor and the sick people. He taught them many good things, like loving your neighbor and being kind. Everyone started to like him — everyone except the warlords. The warlords wanted to get rid of him.

One day Saint Patrick was on his way to preach. His chauffeur was driving the cart when the chauffeur said, "I'm kind of tired, would you mind driving for me?"

Saint Patrick said, "I'll be glad to."

And so they switched places.

A warlord saw the cart and thought that it was Saint Patrick who was sleeping. By mistake he stuck a spear into the sleeping chauffeur. That is how God saved Saint Patrick's life once again.

The Irish people liked to hear about the Bible, but there were a few things they didn't understand. For instance, some people couldn't understand how there could be three Persons in one God. But Saint Patrick was clever. He showed them a clover — you know, a shamrock. He said, "This is one stem, but it has three leaves on it." He touched each leaf to show God the Father, God the Son, and God the Holy Spirit. Then everyone understood a little better. That's why we have shamrocks on Saint Patrick's Day, to remind us.

In the end, Saint Patrick became the patron saint of Ireland. He loved God and helped the Irish to love God. too. He loved people and the people loved him.

Before he died, God sent him one last vision. In his vision Saint Patrick was on top of a mountain. From the mountaintop he saw all the people in Ireland he had helped, and they seemed to be smiling and saying, "Thanks."

What would you pray to Saint Patrick for, now that you know him better?

Prayers to Saint Patrick

Thank you, Saint Patrick, for teaching so well. I do hope that heaven is swell. It was very nice of you to come. You were very clever and not dumb. I will pray to you from this day on.

— Martin

Saint Patrick, I would like to be more Christianlike, but whenever I try to be good I always end up horrible. Please help me to be nicer to my friends and especially to my brothers and sisters. I know you can help because you changed from not knowing what God was, to a saint. You listened to God and did what he told you, and God saved your life. I would appreciate it if you would help. Amen.

— Clare

Dear Saint Patrick, I am Irish, so you are a special saint to me. Please stop all the wars and killing going on in Ireland. For the children's sake, help the grown-ups to make peace.

— Megan

Dear Saint Patrick, you are a loving man. If you were only my teacher, it would be exciting. I like the way you explain things. I love you.

— Joy

4
Saint Cecilia

When Saint Cecilia was a little girl she could play every musical instrument perfectly. Just by touching a harp or a flute she knew exactly how it worked. I guess her friends thought it was some kind of magic. Only Saint Cecilia knew it wasn't magical at all.

Cecilia said that every day she heard the angels singing. Sometimes they would sing a joyful song of praise to God. Sometimes they would sing a sad song because people were offending God. Whatever the angels sang, Saint Cecilia would copy the melody and put it to music.

As Saint Cecilia grew up, she would often entertain her parents after dinner or on a Sunday afternoon. They loved to just sit back, relax, and listen. But Saint Cecilia had a secret dream. She wanted to thank God for blessing her with special musical talent. She wanted to find an instrument that matched the voices of the angels. Searching for just the right sound, she would practice on every single kind of equipment. She tried harps, horns, and flutes, but nothing came close.

So, one day Saint Cecilia decided to invent a brand new musical instrument. She worked and worked to get the perfect sound. When she got it just right, she had created a new instrument — the organ. It sounded like a whole chorus of angels; and Saint Cecilia probably prayed, "Oh God, I hope you like the organ. Every time someone plays it I will be thanking You for being so good to me. I hope it makes You happy whenever You hear it."

Saint Cecilia loved God very much. But not everybody around her felt that way.

The time was shortly after the crucifixion of Jesus. The place was Rome. Saint Cecilia had to keep her love for God a secret, especially since her father was a Roman senator. Her father held a high place of honor within the Roman government. Anyone who was a Christian was despised and put to death.

Back then, the Romans didn't believe in one God. They were mostly pagans, and they had a whole bunch of gods. Christian teachings were totally different from what the pagans were taught. The Christians believed in *one* God, and they believed in loving your enemies the way Jesus Christ did. Pagans considered that a ridiculous idea. I guess they were afraid of it. Maybe that is why some pagans hated Christians.

Anyhow, Saint Cecilia had to be very careful. She had to hide the fact that she was a Christian. Whenever she wanted to pray or go to Mass, she had to meet secretly in a place called the catacombs. That's where Christians in Rome buried their dead. The catacombs are an underground graveyard that's like a maze, and it's very, very dark. Everybody who met there had to use a candle or a torch to see where they were going. Saint Cecilia went to this place all the time to be with her friends and talk about Jesus.

Eventually, the time came when Saint Cecilia was ready to be married, so a suitable husband was picked. Her father decided that a wealthy young politician named Valerian would be just right.

Valerian was well known in Rome as a person who spoke out against "this Christianity nonsense," as he called it. He didn't know anything about Jesus Christ, and he didn't want to know.

One thing Valerian did know for sure was that he loved Saint Cecilia very much, and he was so proud when she became his wife.

Shortly after they were married, Saint Cecilia had to tell her husband about her religious beliefs. She could no longer hide her love for Christ. Valerian didn't like the idea very much, but he never stopped her from going to the prayer meetings or to Mass.

Occasionally, Valerian probably gave Saint Cecilia a hard time for being a Christian. And she probably gave him a hard time for not being one. She really wanted him to love Jesus, because without that they wouldn't have much in common. Maybe she told him, "Just once, please go to this meeting we're having about God."

Tired of this constant demand, Valerian tried to outsmart her. "OK, I'll go," he said. "But I won't believe all this is true unless I see one of the angels you're always talking about."

Saint Cecilia told Valerian the directions to the catacombs and Valerian went. He wasn't too happy about going, but once he was there he got pretty excited about everything he learned. Hearing about one loving God and about the sacrifices of Jesus, Valerian began to understand. At last Christianity made sense to him.

After the meeting Valerian went to Saint Cecilia's room to tell her that he was home and that he liked learning about Jesus. When he opened her door, there was a tremendous surprise waiting for him.

Standing next to Saint Cecilia was an angel, the most beautiful sight Valerian had ever seen. The angel was holding two crowns. One crown was made of lilies which the angel placed on Saint Cecilia's head. The other crown was made of roses which he placed on Valerian's head. From that moment on, Valerian believed. He promised to become a disciple of Christ.

Giving up his brilliant political career, Valerian turned to teaching, and he never hid his newly found faith. He bravely preached to all who would listen. He talked openly in the parks, on the streets, and even in pagan temples. Valerian wanted everybody to learn about the one true God. Saint Cecilia must have been proud of his courage.

Valerian's openness was not appreciated by the pagans. He was getting people really mad. One day the governor decided to stop him and put an end to his religious sermons. The governor ordered his men to kill Valerian on the street, for all to see.

Hearing the news of her husband's death nearly broke Saint Cecilia's heart. She knew that the governor wasn't putting Christian people to death only because they broke the law. Killing was also his way of taking their possessions and keeping them for himself. He made it all seem very legal.

Saint Cecilia also knew that the governor planned to have her executed, too. It was just a matter of time. Before that happened, Saint Cecilia wanted her money to go where it would do the most good. It was then that she prayed, "My dear Lord, I know that the governor is going to kill me, but please don't let him do it until I can give all my money to the poor and suffering. Oh God, find a way to save me until then."

Shortly afterward, the governor accused Cecilia of being a Christian, and he ordered her to prove her innocence. He said, "I will save your life if you give presents to all my gods." He knew she would never do it.

Saint Cecilia couldn't even imagine doing such a thing. She said: "I have one God and only to Him will I offer gifts."

For refusing to cooperate, the governor ordered Cecilia to be suffocated. They tried to drown her, but Saint Cecilia survived. God was with her.

Next, the governor ordered that her head be cut off with a sword. Every time the guard tried to land his blade on her neck, his arm would suddenly stop just in time. The guard tried three times before he managed to wound Cecilia.

It was a serious wound, though. Saint Cecilia managed to live long enough to give her money and jewelry away. Then she said one final prayer of thanks before she died.

"Thank You, heavenly Father, for allowing me to share my wealth with those who really need it. I can't wait to be with You."

Now Saint Cecilia is in heaven, probably making music with the angels. She will always be one of my favorite saints. I love music too, and I know she will help me when I have trouble with my guitar lessons. I may even try the organ.

What would you pray to Saint Cecilia for, now that you know her better?

Prayers to Saint Cecilia

Dear Saint Cecilia, I hope when I die I go up to
heaven, and you can teach me all the musical
instruments. I think we could be friends.

— Ivan

Help us not to have prejudices in the world because of
our religion or color. We aren't thrown to the lions like
some Christians in your time, but sometimes it hurts
just as bad.

— Nancy

Dear Saint Cecilia, could you please help me with my
violin lessons? Every time it just sounds horrible, and
the music comes out scratchy. I sure would appreciate
it.

— Martin

Dear Saint Cecilia, please help me bring out my
special talent that so many people have told me I have,
but I don't seem to recognize. Maybe I can use it to do
something nice for God too.

— Adrienne

5
Saint Nicholas

When Saint Nicholas was a little boy, he shared all of his toys and gifts happily. His parents were really wealthy, and they bought wonderful things for him. No matter what he got, he shared with his friends.

Saint Nicholas was always looking for ways to help people. He became a priest after his mother and father died, and, little by little, he gave all of his riches away. I think it made him happy to make other people happy.

Once he went to buy some bread and cheese for lunch. While he was walking into the supermarket, he heard two wealthy men talking on the street. They were saying that it was a shame their friend Osman was not able to afford a wedding for his daughters.

"Poor old Osman lost all his money," one man said. "Now his daughters will never be able to marry."

"Sure is a pity," the other fellow said. "They just don't have any money to buy a husband."

"That's right!" the other man replied. "No dowry, no husband."

Now Saint Nicholas was curious. He knew exactly where Osman lived, and he decided to pay him a visit. You see, it wasn't a big city like New York or Chicago, where you can't possibly know everybody! This was just a quiet town in Turkey that seemed more like a small neighborhood. And, because Saint Nicholas was the parish priest, he knew just where to go.

That night after dinner, Nicholas went to Osman's house and peeked in the window. He saw Osman and his three daughters sitting around in the living room, talking. When it was time for them to go to bed, Saint Nicholas watched as the old man smiled and kissed each of his girls good-night. But Saint Nicholas could tell that, inside, Osman was really worried and upset. When the girls left the room, the poor man had a troubled frown all over his face. Maybe he was feeling like a failure or something.

Then Saint Nicholas had a terrific idea. "I'll just surprise the three daughters and give them some money myself! But I better be careful that nobody finds out, or else it won't be a surprise."

The next night, when everybody went off to bed, Saint Nicholas crept silently up to Osman's living room window. This time, instead of just looking around, Nicholas took a bag of gold coins from his pocket and threw them through the open window.

The next morning nobody suspected what had happened. As usual, the oldest daughter went to get her stockings that were hanging from the fireplace. She washed her stockings every night, and the fireplace was the only spot where they would dry. You know, they didn't have washers and driers like we do now. Anyway, inside one of the stockings she found the gold coins.

"Oh boy!" she said. "Now I can get married. I have a gift to give to my future husband!"

"I wonder who put that money there," one of the other sisters said.

"Do you think it was your boyfriend?" the third sister asked.

"I don't know," replied the oldest girl. "But whoever it was sure has made me happy." And she ran off to tell her boyfriend the good news.

That night, Saint Nicholas returned to do the same thing all over again. He tossed some more gold coins

through the window. The next day the second daughter began to clean the house. All of a sudden she got very excited. Under a chair she found the money.

"I don't believe it!" she said. "Now I can get married, too."

Then the girls ran to their father and said, "You must be the one who's leaving all this money around.

What a fantastic surprise. You were just teasing when you said that you couldn't afford a dowry. Daddy, you are wonderful.''

Then the second daughter ran off to tell her boyfriend, too.

Now Osman was getting all mixed up. He knew he didn't have money to leave just lying around the house. In fact, he barely had any money at all. So he decided to stay up and hide behind the bushes in front of the house. "I'll stay up all night if I have to," he thought. "I just have to catch the person who is doing this."

That night Osman saw. Saint Nicholas came back just like before.

As usual, Nicholas reached in his pocket for the gold coins. Then he threw them in the window for the third daughter. But this time Osman caught him red-handed.

"Oh, Father Nicholas! So you are the one who has been tossing all that money in my house."

"Well, you caught me," Saint Nicholas said. "But please don't tell anybody. Let it be our little secret."

Osman replied, "OK, I promise not to say a word. But I have to thank you. You have made us all so very happy."

Finally, the next morning the third daughter found her money too, and all three girls were able to be married.

I guess Saint Nicholas always saved some spare cash just in case someone needed his help. He never really wore a disguise like Santa Claus, but this is how the Santa Claus legend started.

Saint Nicholas also had something happen to him that happened to Jesus. One time Nicholas was on his way to the Holy Land. That's where Jesus grew up. It was a long trip, and Nicholas had to travel by boat. All of a sudden, before he knew what hit him, a huge storm started to shake the sea. Everybody was really scared. There were tidal waves, and the wind was blowing rain. The sky was dark and very cloudy. Then the sails on the boat split in half. The people just couldn't take it anymore.

"We are all going to drown," they screamed.

So, Saint Nicholas prayed a special prayer. "Oh my God, we need Your help. Please calm things down." Something inside him told Nicholas to stand up and tell the wind to stop blowing and the rain to stop raining. When he did it, the weather settled down and became still, just like the time Jesus did it with Peter and the apostles.

Because he performed the miracle to stop the storm and calm the sea, Saint Nicholas became the patron saint for sailors. And because he loved kids and provided the three daughters with a dowry, he became the protector of children.

What would you pray to Saint Nicholas for, now that you know him better?

Prayers to Saint Nicholas

Dear Saint Nicholas, help me share a little better with my brother because my mom says I have to try harder.

— Anthony

Dear Saint Nicholas, some people are rich, and they don't care about other people. They want to keep everything for themselves and say "I don't care." But you cared, because you gave everything away. You were so generous, because you helped those girls get married by giving them money. I'm glad we don't have to buy husbands anymore. Help me be like you.

— Linda

Dear Saint Nicholas, I like to go sailing with my dad. Sometimes the waves get high, and I get really scared. Please watch over us when we are in the boat.

— Jamie

Saint Nick, it's OK that you didn't bring me a real horse for Christmas. I think I like the Atari game better anyhow.

— Chris

6
Saint Elizabeth
of Hungary

When Saint Elizabeth was a little girl, she was very lonely. Unlike most children, she never knew her brothers or sisters. She wasn't even raised by her own mother and father. I guess she hardly knew them. It was all kind of complicated.

You see, during this time, Saint Elizabeth's father was king of Hungary; and he was always busy fighting wars. Hoping to settle Hungary's problems, Elizabeth's father the king made a bargain with the ruler of another country. The agreement was that the two countries would be united through marriage. Saint Elizabeth's father promised the ruler that Elizabeth would marry the ruler's son, Louis. Kings were always settling things that way.

Even though it was hard to say good-bye, Elizabeth's parents decided not to wait until she grew up to send her away. When she was only four years old, Saint Elizabeth was forced to move in with her new family. That way everybody could get acquainted. "Besides, she has to learn the customs and language of this foreign country," her father thought.

There were two wonderful things about Saint Elizabeth that made her special. She was both kind and beautiful. Unfortunately, these two things made her new life very difficult and lonely.

Except for Louis, the ruler's son, it was really hard for Elizabeth to find a friend. Nobody made her feel welcome. All the people who lived in the castle were jealous. Often they told lies about Elizabeth and talked behind her back. It seems like they wanted to hurt her feelings so that she would go back where she came from. But Saint Elizabeth made the best of it and stayed.

Instead of being angry with these people, Elizabeth tried even harder to be more cheerful and helpful. It was no use. No matter how hard she tried, no one seemed to like her.

Saint Elizabeth would turn to God for comfort and company. She prayed every day and built a special friendship with Him. Maybe she said, "Oh God, I really don't mind anything that happens in this castle because I know You are always with me."

Elizabeth's friend, Louis, tried to be with her as much as possible. But Louis was often away on business trips. Whenever he came back, though, he would bring Elizabeth candy or jewels and clothes. That was Louis's way of telling Elizabeth how much he loved her. Even though he was a lot older than she, Louis was glad that Saint Elizabeth was going to be his wife. Through the years they grew to love each other more and more. They understood each other.

Finally, Saint Elizabeth was old enough to be married. As a grown-up she was even more beautiful than ever before, and Louis was proud to be her husband.

After the wedding, Saint Elizabeth kept very busy helping the poor and needy of the kingdom. If someone was hungry, Elizabeth would go to the kitchen in the castle and give the person some food. Maybe she would provide a whole loaf of bread and big chunks of cheese. If she met an elderly couple who were too old to get around, Saint Elizabeth would do their housework and shopping or anything else they needed. If a family had a sick child, she would nurse the youngster back to health. No matter who it was or what it was, Saint Elizabeth did all that she could.

These good works didn't go unnoticed. The wealthy people of the court were getting fed up. "We have to find a way to get rid of this pest," they said. They tried to get her in trouble with Louis, and a couple of times they almost did.

"She's giving all our food away," they complained. "She took all the bread from the kitchen and went out and gave it to the poor. These are hard times for everyone. We barely have enough bread for ourselves.''

On and on they went, and for the first time Louis was really angry. ''Enough with this constant charity,'' he thought. ''I must stop it before it gets out of hand.''

Marching right out of the castle, Louis found Elizabeth walking down a dirt road. She could see that he was unusually upset and really mad.

''Open your coat!'' Louis demanded.

As she untied her coat, God protected her. Instead of bread, Louis only saw a whole bunch of roses fall out. Then her face glowed in a heavenly way. God was giving Louis a sign that Saint Elizabeth was doing the right thing and that she should not be punished. So Louis walked Elizabeth home. He felt ashamed for doubting his wife.

When they saw that Louis's attitude had changed, the noble people were furious. They decided to try even harder to ruin Saint Elizabeth.

One day when Louis was coming home from work, someone told him that Elizabeth had brought home a dirty old leper. Everyone was afraid of lepers. That's when your skin falls off; and if you touch somebody who has it, then you'll get it too.

''And, to make matters worse,'' the spy said, ''she even put the diseased person in *your* bed!''

Hearing this, Louis ran up the stairs and into his bedroom. Once again, he was furious. ''This finally has gone too far,'' Louis said to himself. ''How could she put a leper in our bed?''

In the bedroom, Louis rushed to the bed and pulled back the covers. Instead of a leper, he was surprised to see something amazing. Lying upon his bed was the vision of Jesus Christ on the Cross. At that moment Louis knew that Elizabeth was indeed a saint. He promised never to interfere with her good works again.

From then on, Louis and Saint Elizabeth were very happy together — that is, until one day when Louis went away to fight in the wars known as the Crusades. Louis never came back. He got a sickness called the plague which was caused and carried by rats. Louis died.

When Saint Elizabeth heard the news, her heart was broken. With God's help, she got through the ordeal and carried on. After Louis's death, though, Elizabeth never felt the same. She simply felt empty inside.

Soon, her ambitious brother-in-law was afraid that Elizabeth would take over as ruler. He decided to send her away to live in a convent, and she didn't argue.

While she was there in the convent, a man named Conrad gave Elizabeth a pretty hard time. Even though she was a queen, Conrad made her life miserable. If he thought Elizabeth was doing something wrong, Conrad would slap her and hit her with a stick. He even fired all her maids and hired people to spy on her constantly. Every little thing she did, Conrad wanted to know about it. Saint Elizabeth had no privacy, but she never got mad by yelling and screaming. She simply did her job as best she could.

Always, Saint Elizabeth kept on praying daily to God for help. But she didn't pray for herself. She cared about other people's needs. Even though she was a princess and could have gone back to her father's castle in Hungary, she stayed to comfort the poor and helpless. Saint Elizabeth started hospitals for people who couldn't afford a doctor. She started shelters for people who were homeless. She even went fishing so that a hungry family could have something to eat.

Before she died, Saint Elizabeth gave all her jewels and money away. At the age of twenty-four, Elizabeth joined her beloved husband, Louis, in heaven. She probably died because she worked too hard.

What would you pray to Saint Elizabeth for, now that you know her better?

Prayers to Saint Elizabeth

Dear Saint Elizabeth,
  You are so young,
  Yet you help the poor.
  You are so hurt,
  Yet you do not fear.
Help me.

— Kim

Dear Saint Elizabeth, can you help me when I go fishing? Amen.

— Anthony

Dear Saint Elizabeth, so smart and bright, please help us to do the same as you did and help us to give up for others and become followers of God. To love those who hate us. To love those who are angry at us. To love the sick with bad diseases. And to love God more and more every day.

— Colm

Dear Saint Elizabeth, can you help me be like you? To help the poor and sick and elderly? Sometimes I'm too busy having fun to help old people, but not you. You were different. Please help me take time, too.

— Jennifer

7
Saint Anthony
of Padua

When Saint Anthony was a little boy, he talked very softly. He was a short, chubby kid, and nobody seemed to notice him. I guess his small size made him kind of shy, too, because he never really had that much to say.

Often he wondered what our Lord wanted him to do with his life when he grew up. "Oh God," he prayed, "please tell me how I can serve You."

Nobody dreamed — not even the timid little saint — that God had something very special planned for him. When the time came, Saint Anthony would have his answer.

Even though his parents were very wealthy, Saint Anthony decided to give up all the things that money could buy and join the Franciscan Order. Saint Francis of Assisi started this group, the Franciscans, for men who promised to be poor, humble, and, most of all, helpful to the needy. Saint Anthony always admired Saint Francis, and he hoped to follow his example.

In case you've never seen a Franciscan friar, they always wear brown robes with hoods on them. Franciscans used to shave a bald spot on top of their heads, but they were allowed to wear short hair on the sides.

Anyhow, Saint Anthony wore the friar outfit and lived with a bunch of other friars. Most of the time he kept to himself, praying. His job was to do the dishes when everybody had finished eating. He washed every single plate, pot, and pan after each meal and never complained.

This went on for several years until something strange happened that changed Saint Anthony's life forever.

One day there was a graduation ceremony for some new Brothers. Someone was supposed to give a speech to welcome them into the group. But then, somehow, things got all mixed up. Nobody knew who was supposed to give the speech, and everyone just looked around the room, waiting. This must have been very embarrassing.

So, the head friar called Saint Anthony over to his table and said, "Look, we really have a problem here. Someone has got to say something, and I'm picking you."

Now, Saint Anthony was very surprised because no one had ever asked him to speak before. He didn't have much experience in getting up in front of a group of people. "I don't know what to say," he said. "I haven't prepared a speech or anything."

But the friar had a pretty good feeling that Anthony was right for the job. "Don't worry, Brother Anthony," he answered calmly. "Make up something. I know the Holy Spirit will guide you."

As Saint Anthony stood up to speak, some of the Brothers were probably yawning and shifting around. Everyone was expecting a boring speech, and they looked like they just wanted to get the whole thing over with so they could leave.

As Saint Anthony spoke, the years of silence seemed to be broken. All the men in the room couldn't wait to hear more. They were spellbound. Saint Anthony told them about God's love for them and how each man was important to our Lord. When he finished, you could have heard a pin drop in the room. It was that quiet. Anthony's speech was so beautiful that everyone was amazed at what they had heard.

"I had no idea that Brother Anthony could speak so well," one friar said.

"He always seemed so shy," another replied.

Soon all the villagers and townspeople heard of Saint Anthony's gift for talking. Everybody wanted to hear what he had to say. Crowds started to pour into the little Franciscan chapel. It was packed with people sitting, standing, and waiting outside.

Some folks would wake up really early before work and go to the Mass that Saint Anthony celebrated. Some would even spend the night in church to make sure they got a seat. Eventually, everybody had to go outside so that the crowd could have a chance to hear.

Saint Anthony's words seemed to change their lives. People wanted to be near him. Sinners would change and be good. People would stop quarreling and settle things. Thieves would stop stealing and return the things they took.

Saint Anthony had a special effect on everyone, or almost everyone. There was one man who thought the whole thing was absurd. He didn't even believe in God.

"I'll only believe if my donkey goes out of the stable and kneels before the Eucharist. Fat chance that will ever happen," he laughed.

A few days later Saint Anthony had to bring the sacraments to a sick man who was unable to get out of bed and go to Mass. All of a sudden the donkey saw Saint Anthony walking, and the donkey trotted off to kneel in front of Anthony as he passed by bringing Communion. Of course, the man who didn't believe in God saw this happen too, and from that day on the man believed.

Another time something else unusual occurred. A young friar borrowed Saint Anthony's Psalm book without asking. Because Saint Anthony traveled around so much, he thought he had lost the book somewhere. "When I can, I'll look for it," he thought.

But the whole time the young friar kept the book, he had funny feelings about it. He started having horrible nightmares, and he broke out in a cold sweat. He couldn't wait to tell Saint Anthony what he had done and return the book.

Afterward, when he had returned the book, the troubled friar felt normal again.

That's why you should pray to Saint Anthony if you ever lose anything. He can help get it back for you.

Once when I lost my homework, Saint Anthony helped. I looked for the homework everywhere, and I was really getting worried. I looked in my bag, in the closets and drawers, everywhere. Suddenly, I just stopped searching and asked Saint Anthony for help. The next day I found the homework in my friend's house. It just goes to show you what Saint Anthony can do.

Saint Anthony is one of my favorite saints — not just because he helps me find things but because he made other people feel close to God. Even though it was hard for him to talk in front of people, he did it. Maybe God was the one doing all the talking through Saint Anthony. He must be pretty special, don't you think?

What would you pray to Saint Anthony for, now that you know him better?

Prayers to Saint Anthony

Dear Saint Anthony, can you help me find my shoes because there is a dance on Friday? My shoes are white with gold ribbons. Thank you.

— Wendy

Dear Saint Anthony, I wish you were still alive and could be someone I know. I would have liked to hear all the wonderful things you talked about. Maybe I could learn more about Jesus by talking with you. Someday maybe we could meet.

— Barbara

Oh Saint Anthony, you were really great. Please help me to be more like you. Even though I'm kind of shy like you, I would like to be able to talk to people. Amen.

— Mike

8
Saint Bernadette

When Saint Bernadette was a little girl, she was very sickly. The doctor said she had asthma. Late at night, when the rest of her family were sleeping comfortably in bed, Saint Bernadette would be awake coughing, wheezing, and gasping for air. I guess it's kind of like suffocating. No matter how hard she tried, she could hardly breathe.

When this happened, Saint Bernadette wanted to be considerate and deal with the problem by herself. Her parents had enough troubles of their own.

Most of the time Saint Bernadette's father was out of work. At best, he could only find odd jobs in the small town of Lourdes, France, where the family lived.

Early each morning, Bernadette's father left home, hoping to find some kind of work. Money was badly needed to pay the bills and provide food for his very large family. There were eleven children.

Knocking on all kinds of doors, the desperate father would do anything. Sometimes he hauled trash for rich villagers. Sometimes he scrubbed hospital floors or delivered bread for the local bakery. That's only if he was lucky. Days or weeks would go by when he was just another poor man on the streets, needing a job.

Doctors and medicine were luxuries he couldn't afford. So, every time Saint Bernadette had an asthma attack, she simply suffered quietly, waiting for it to end. Often she said the rosary during this time, and the Blessed Mother filled her thoughts.

The asthma was a constant problem, and Bernadette was absent a lot from school. No matter how hard she tried, Saint Bernadette couldn't catch up with the rest of her class. It seemed that she was always being held back in the second grade.

Going to school was often worse than being sick. Lessons were bad enough, but the other kids gave Bernadette a pretty rough time. Some classmates would be embarrassed for her, but others laughed whenever she answered the teacher's questions. Saint Bernadette tried to cope with it all because she wanted to make her First Communion more than anything else in the whole world. For so many years she had failed religion class. Now she was determined to pass. Finally, at the age of fourteen, she did pass.

Except for her family, the only thing that made Saint Bernadette happy was saying the rosary. She felt a special kind of peace and joy whenever she thought of Mary. Without knowing it, the Blessed Mother was about to pay Bernadette a visit and change her life forever.

One chilly afternoon, Saint Bernadette's mother needed some firewood to warm the house. She called two of her daughters into the living room and said, "Go quickly and find some firewood before it gets dark. I need it right away."

Anxious to do something useful, Saint Bernadette begged to go too. "Please, Mother, let me help. I'll dress warmly and take it easy."

Reluctantly, the worried mother said OK.

Once outside, the three sisters walked slowly, but Saint Bernadette had a tough time keeping up. She started falling behind, and her sisters were getting annoyed. "Come on, Bernadette. We haven't got all day, you know."

The place where they had to get the firewood was somewhere around the town dump, where Saint Bernadette's father often hauled garbage. The air was

stale, and it really smelled bad. It was especially awful for Saint Bernadette. She was very sensitive to things like that, but she didn't complain or let on that she was having trouble.

When they finally arrived at the right place, the younger sister noticed that the best wood lay across a stream. "Wait here," the sisters told Bernadette. "The last thing we need is for you to get wet feet."

Knowing they were right, Saint Bernadette stayed behind and decided to say the rosary. Taking the beads from her pocket, she started to make the Sign of the Cross. Suddenly, Bernadette noticed a brilliant light glowing softly from the grotto. A grotto is like a small cave on the side of a hill.

Normally shy, Saint Bernadette would have been afraid. But this time she was bravely curious. Drawing her nearer and nearer, the light seemed loving and warm. As she got closer, the light changed into a beautiful lady dressed in white with a blue belt. The lady's smiling face was kind with the loveliest eyes Saint Bernadette had ever seen.

At first the lady and Bernadette probably just got acquainted. Maybe the lady asked, "Are you feeling better?" and "How are you doing in school?" Saint Bernadette answered the questions, and together they said the rosary.

By the time her sisters were finished with their chore, they found Saint Bernadette kneeling in front of the trashy grotto. Something was strange. "Bernadette looks different," one of the sisters commented. "I hope she's not getting sick again," the other worried.

Rambling on and on about what happened, Saint Bernadette couldn't stop talking all the way home. Keeping well ahead of her sisters, not once did she lose her breath.

That night during dinner, Saint Bernadette talked constantly about the lady. "What would a beautiful lady be doing in the dump?" her sisters joked. Nobody could make any sense of it.

Saint Bernadette really didn't mind the teasing. Her lady in white promised to return, and she could hardly wait.

Eventually, people heard rumors of the vision and started to follow Bernadette. "Maybe there is something to this lady," people thought. Whenever this young girl knelt in front of the grotto, everybody was aware of a strange silence. People were curious and confused. They said things like, "If the lady is from heaven, ask her for a miracle. Bernadette, we need a sign." They wanted to be sure the whole thing was true. Even the parish priest wanted to know the lady's name. Saint Bernadette promised that she would ask.

On the very last visit, the miracle happened — but not the way everybody thought it would.

The lady told Saint Bernadette to dig a hole in the ground and drink from the river.

"Oh, you mean the stream?" Saint Bernadette asked.

"No," the lady answered. "Dig from the earth and a river will flow."

As Saint Bernadette began to scoop out the dirt, the ground became a muddy mess. Obediently, Bernadette tried to drink. As she did, the townspeople started to laugh and make fun of her. "Ha!" they said. "Is that our miracle? A young girl with mud all over her face?"

Embarrassed, Bernadette's mother tried to protect her by dragging her home. As the mother and daughter pushed through the crowds, the abuse continued. There was no miracle. The people felt betrayed. "Bernadette has played a terrible trick on us," they shouted. "All she wanted was to be famous."

On her way home, Bernadette insisted on stopping off at the rectory, where the priest lived. Saint Bernadette told the priest that the lady had said, ''I am the Immaculate Conception.'' Saint Bernadette didn't really understand what that meant, but her priest knew all too well. The lady in white was the Blessed Mother of our Lord. All along, Saint Bernadette had been visiting with her Lady of the Rosary.

When everything settled down and all the people had deserted the grotto, a wonderful miracle did happen.

A river appeared on the very spot where Saint Bernadette had been digging. Our Lady hadn't let her down after all. Accidently, a blind man stumbled and fell into the river. But the man didn't drown. Instead, the first miracle occurred. Rubbing the water from his face, the blind man opened his eyes. He could see. The first sight he saw in his whole life was the miraculous river he was standing in. Quickly, the man rushed into town to tell everybody about the water's healing powers. To this day, people from all over the world come to that river. They bring their sick and dying, and the water makes them well.

The Blessed Mother also gave Saint Bernadette a message for all the world to hear. ''Tell everyone to say their rosary and to pray for sinners. People must love God again and stop offending Him.''

Soon Saint Bernadette became very famous. Everyone wanted to talk to her. Even though she felt shy around strangers, she never turned anyone away. Exhausted, she told the story of her visions over and over again. Sometimes her new friends wanted to buy her presents, but Saint Bernadette always refused.

When she was old enough, Bernadette decided to be

a nun. It was hard to leave her family and the town where she grew up, but she realized that this would make the Blessed Mother happy.

After she was in the convent for a short time, Bernadette became very sick again. So, the other Sisters let her become a nun ahead of time. Even though she was weak, she worked in the hospital and scrubbed floors in the convent. It was hard, but she didn't argue. She seemed happy to do it, every day, until she died.

Saint Bernadette will always be a special saint to me. I admire her, not just because she was so sickly and never complained but also because she was so very close to our Blessed Lady.

What would you pray to Saint Bernadette for, now that you know her better?

Prayers to Saint Bernadette

Dear Saint Bernadette, please help the people who sin and steal. I know you were a very holy saint. I hope you can help all the people who are not well and who are suffering. I would like to ask you a favor. Could you help my father? He is sick. And help my mother, too. Amen.

— Monica

Dear Saint Bernadette, I think you're very special because you saw our Holy Mother. Since you're so special I would like to ask you something. Saint Bernadette, help my mom get a job and bless her. Amen.

— Patricia

Saint Bernadette, I hope you're having a nice time in heaven, because I am having a nice time down here. You deserve it. Your friend,

— Michelle

Dear Saint Bernadette, I will pray to you whenever I am sick or need help in school or at home. Thanks for being a good example for us.

— Amy

Bibliography

Butler, Alban. *Lives of the Saints*. Four-volume reprint of the 1956 edition. Christian Classics, 1962.

Farmer, David Hugh, ed. *The Oxford Dictionary of Saints*. Oxford University Press, 1978.

Ferguson, George. *Signs and Symbols in Christian Art*. Oxford University Press, 1969.

Post, W. Ellwood. *Saints, Signs and Symbols*. Morehouse-Barlow Company, 1974.

Wittemore, Carroll E., ed. *Symbols of the Church*. Abingdon Press, 1959.

MORE BOOKS FOR CHILDREN

BEDTIME STORIES OF THE SAINTS: Books One and Two
The lives of saints told in children's language. These short stories include St. Joseph, St. Joan of Arc, St. Paul, St. Martin de Porres, and others. $1.95 each

HOW YOU LIVE WITH JESUS: Catechism for Today's Young Catholic
Basic, compact, comprehensive, with colorful illustrations and simple explanations. For the middle grades and older. Contains workshop sections, mini-tests, and guide notes for parents and teachers. $3.50   Teacher's Guide — $4.95

MEETING THE FORGIVING JESUS: A Child's Book for First Penance
Presents a basic, positive approach to preparation for First Penance. Helps the child understand the basics of the sacrament, recognize the need for Penance, experience Penance as a peace-filled celebration. $1.75   Teacher's Guide — $2.95

MEETING JESUS IN HOLY COMMUNION:
A Child's Book for First Eucharist
Gives young Catholics a deeper understanding of the Eucharist and helps them grow in awareness of Jesus as our Bread of Life. Includes: Words to Know, Mini-tests, Prayers for Before and After Communion. $1.75   Teacher's Guide — $3.95

IN MY HEART ROOM: Sixteen Love Prayers for Little Children
A book to be used by parent and child to teach children how to pray in a special way (concentration and meditation). A companion coloring book that includes Scripture quotes and tear-out pages that make posters is also available. $1.50 each

Order from your local bookstore or write to:
Liguori Publications, Box 060, Liguori, Missouri 63057
*(Please add 50¢ postage and handling for first item
ordered and 25¢ for each additional item.)*